746.3

CRAFT AND ART

TAPESTRY

Copyright © by SPADEM, Paris; ADAGP, Paris; COSMOPRESS, Geneva

© Les Editions de Bonvent SA, Geneva 1971.

Library of Congress Catalog Card Number: 73-4865
ISBN 0-442-29993-1

Printed in Switzerland.

Published in 1974 by Van Nostrand Reinhold Company Inc., 450 West 33rd Street, New York
N.Y. 10001 and Van Nostrand Reinhold Company Ltd., 25–28 Buckingham Gate, London
SW1E 6LQ.

Van Nostrand Reinhold Company Regional Offices:
New York, Cincinnati, Chicago, Millbrae, Dallas.
Van Nostrand Reinhold Company International Offices:
London, Toronto, Melbourne.

CRAFT AND ART

Maurice Pianzola
Julien Coffinet

TAPESTRY

VAN NOSTRAND REINHOLD COMPANY
VNR
New York · Cincinnati · Toronto · London · Melbourne

Guajira woman weaving

CONTENTS

1 PENELOPE AND ARACHNE

Preparing the leashes

It seems as if that good and faithful lady Penelope – and who can avoid thinking of her on opening this book, written in praise of the shrewd weaver faithful to an art many thousands of years old – it certainly seems as if Odysseus' wife had before her a high-warp loom – and here we are already involved with technical terms – when, as Homer tells us, "She set up a great warp on her loom in the mansion, and wove away, fine work and wide across (...) There she was all day long, working away at the great web; but at night she used to unravel it by torchlight."[1]

As a matter of fact Penelope, in her endless sorrow, was perpetuating the gestures of the presumptuous maiden Arachne, so able a practitioner of her art, "whether, as Ovid says, she was winding the rough yarn upon a new ball, or fingering the stuff, then reaching back to the distaff for more wool, fleecy as a cloud, to draw into long soft threads, or giving a twist with practised thumb to the graceful spindle, or embroidering with her needle: you could know that Pallas had taught her."[2]

A headstrong young woman was Arachne, she refused to acknowledge the goddess' supremacy; her skill was to bring about her downfall:

7

High-warp tapestry workshop at the Gobelins[3]

Arachne weaving[4]

"They both take their separate positions without delay and they stretch the fine warp each upon her loom. The web is bound upon the beam, the reed separates the threads of the warp, the woof is threaded through by the sharp shuttles which their busy fingers ply, the notched teeth of the hammering slay beat the woof into place as it shot between the threads of the web. They speed on the work with their mantles close girt about their breasts and move back and forth their well-trained hands, their eager zeal beguiling their toil. There are interwoven the purple threads dyed in Tyrian kettles, and lighter colours insensibly shading off from these. As when after a storm of rain the sun's rays strike through, and a rainbow, with its huge curve, stains the wide sky, though a thousand different colours shine in it, the eye cannot detect the change from each one to the next; so like appear adjacent colours, but the extremes are plainly different. There, too, they weave in pliant threads of gold, and trace in the weft some ancient tale."

Adding, perhaps, insult to injury, Arachne portrayed the more improper and bucolic of the god's love-affairs, a

none too innocent pastoral, a menagerie, rather, in which bulls, cows, rams, stallions, eagles, swans and serpents embrace shepherds and shepherdesses, and where even the ivy makes love to wayside flowers.

As we know, this earned her being changed into the despised spider, who still patiently decorates our attics with her fine weavings.

Homer, Ovid, Penelope, Arachne . . . references which demonstrate how difficult it is to rid ourselves of a western, European view of things.

In fact tapestry, the art of adorning and giving warmth to walls of habitations and temples by lining them with hangings, was practised by the Egyptians as far back as the XVIIIth dynasty, nearly 2000 years before our era. Wonder-struck descriptions of the tapestries of Babylon and Nineveh have been handed down to us by the writers of Antiquity, but a great many fragments of hangings made by the Copts, Egypt's first Christians, are still in existence; their colours have been preserved by the dry atmosphere of the tombs in which they were buried.

Arachne [5]

The striking colours of pre-Columbian material from Peru have likewise been preserved by the absence of humidity; the earliest examples are from a period that coincides with the beginnings of the Christian era.

Finally, the Chinese wove silken tapestries, the *K'o-sseu* tapestries, during the T'ang Dynasty, from the 7th to the 10th century.

The Syrians invented the interweaving of woolen weft with linen warp, Peruvian fabrics were made from aloe, llama wool or alpaca . . . but the point is that throughout the ages, and from continent to continent, in documents, stories, poems and scenes on painted pottery, we find the same basic loom, a warp of stretched threads into which the coloured threads of the weft are woven.

Jean Boutellis, Ecoute je t'appelle *(fragment) 1970. Saint-Cyr workshop*

2 ARTIST, ARTISAN?

The weaver is a man who is caught between, on the one hand, his loom, a few simple tools and his wool, and on the other hand, the artist, who presents him with a model to copy, or simply places an order.

Is he, then, merely a skillful worker, a technician? The answer must be no, because he has to interpret the artist's model, just as a musician interprets a score. He can of course go further, and become a creative artist in his own right, carrying out his own composition.

The relationship between the artist and the artisan, who collaborate, agree or disagree and sometimes even change roles, the artist becoming a craftsman, the artisan rising to the level of artist, has evolved, while the principle of the loom and the materials scarcely changed until the artistic explosion of the last few years, which has created problems of semantics. Aren't these rough objects, possessing a kind of refined savagery, which have come bursting out of studios no longer to cover walls but to occupy the centre of a room, aren't they more like textile or woven sculptures than tapestry?

We shall, in this book, describe the high-warp technique (vertical loom) and show how it differs from the low-warp (horizontal loom) technique. After which we shall give a brief outline of the history of tapestry in Europe, trying always to relate closely the illustrations to the text.

Gobelins high-warp tapestry. Craftsman ready to start the work[3]

Fig. 1.

15

16

3 HIGH-WARP, LOW-WARP

Tapestry, says the famous French dictionary Robert, is "a work of art in woven material, carried out by hand on the loom, in which the design is made by the weave itself (and not applied), intended to form vertical panels".

The main characteristic of tapestry is that the weft threads pass to and fro on the warp threads which they cover completely both back and front.

It must thus be distinguished from embroidery, such as embroidery on canvas, a type of needlework in which a canvas background is covered with wool or silk threads.

Installed at the high-warp loom (vertical loom) the craftsman has the model or cartoon behind him. Before him is the wrong side of the work, he can see the right side with the help of a mirror.

On a low-warp (horizontal) loom the craftsman works the right way round. The cartoon is placed under the loom. The even and odd warp threads are crossed in turn by pressing on pedals.

Warping
Weaving is necessarily preceded by *warping,* which comprises preparing the warp

Jean Lurçat, Tout Feu, tout Flamme. *1963. Port-alegre workshop*

threads and setting them up on the loom (threads vertical).

The extremely simple practice at the Gobelins and Savonnerie ateliers, is to arrange the threads into groups – know as *piennes* – each of the piennes being the equivalent of 10 cm. (4 inches) width of material.

Two stout wooden pegs are fixed in a horizontal position at a distance apart equal to the length of the piennes to be made up.

Two more similar pegs are fixed in position in the straight line uniting the outside ones. They are used for the *cross*.

The weaver makes a loop at the end of the skein of warp thread, which is on a spool. He slips the loop on one of the outside pegs, and, holding the thread between thumb and forefinger, works towards the cross, where he passes the thread over the first peg and under the second, then moves on to the other outside peg, passes the thread under it, round it, and back towards the cross pegs again, this time going over

The weaver slips a loop onto the outside peg

The threads making up a pienne *are stretched between the pegs. Each thread crosses its neighbours at the cross*

The weaver then ties in, centimetre by centimetre, the string which separates the threads

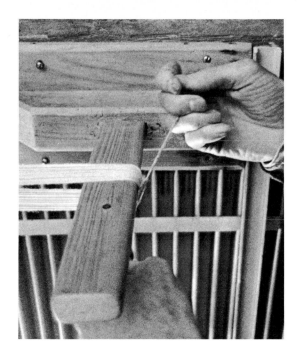

The weaver then knots a string tightly round the cross to hold it in place when the pienne is removed from the pegs

The weaver also knots a string round the threads at both ends

20

the second peg and under the first, and back to the starting point where he goes under and round the peg and starts all over again.

So each return journey makes up two threads. When the number of threads necessary to build up the 10 cm. (4 inches) is attained, the weaver makes a loop and slips it onto the outside peg.

Preparing the piennes is very simple, but in the case of a very long (that is to say, very high) tapestry, a large workshop is called for. Many weavers get round this by using a rectangular frame which has appropriate holes to receive the pegs. Additional pegs can be added to the four mentioned above. They make it possible to zig-zag the length on the piennes through several angles.

The pienne is completed. The weaver removes it from the pegs and plaits it to prevent the threads from becoming tangled

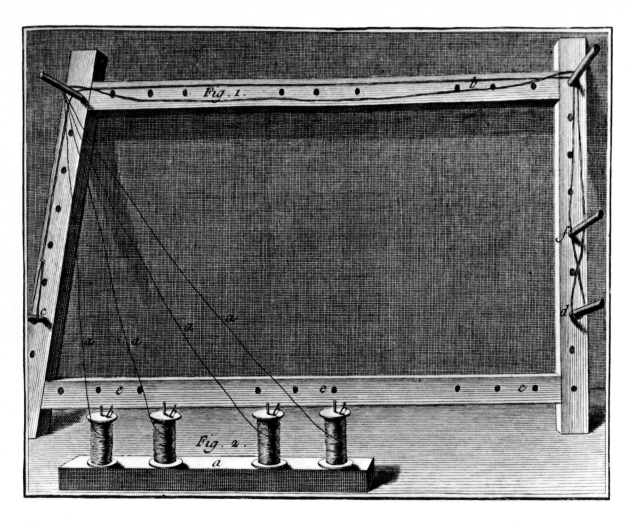

Fig. 1.

Fig. 2.

22

4 THE HIGH-WARP LOOM

Gobelins high-warp tapestry. Warping section: a frame[3]

The piennes are fixed on the beam bar of the upper roller

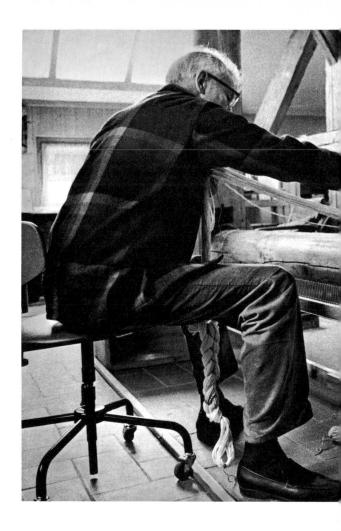

The weaver prepares the reed

*The weaver, helped by an assistant, arranges the warp
threads in the dents of the reed, centimetre by centimetre*

Setting up the loom

When the loom has been set up, the warp threads are stretched evenly between the top and bottom rollers. They are divided into two sets of odd and even numbers by the *cross rod*: the odd threads (known in French as the *fils de croisure*) pass behind the cross rod, the even threads *(fils de lice)* pass in front. The opening between the two sets is called a *shed*. The even threads are held by *leashes (heddles)*, the odd threads remain free.

Weaving is carried out by passing the weft thread through two alternate sheds: the *rod shed*, which is made by pulling back the odd set of warp threads, and the *leash shed* made by pulling back on the leashes. The weft is passed from left to right through the rod shed, and from right to left through the leash shed. A single weft thread is called a *pick*.

Once all the warp threads have been fitted in the dents of the reed, the latter is shut and placed on its supports which are screwed into the uprights of the loom

The beam bar is then fixed in its groove on the upper roller. The separating strings can be seen under the reed, then the knots at the cross, finally the bottom ends of the piennes, still plaited

The piennes are slipped onto the beam bar of the lower roller

The weaver lays a cord over the cross knots. He will then run another cord under the same knots

The cords are attached to the uprights. The cross is thus remade and the knots, now useless, are undone. The separating strings will also be removed

An even thread (fil de lice) is singled out; the weaver passes the bobbin *behind both the cross rod and the fil de lice*

The weaver passes the bobbin with his right hand and grasps it with his left hand

29

*Once a leash is completed two or three knots are made
before moving on to the next leash*

The beam bar is fixed in the groove on the roller by means of screwed plates

Before starting work on a tapestry the weaver weaves
several picks which he attaches to the sides of the loom;
the warp threads are thus prepared for weaving

Seignorial Life *series*. The Bath *(detail)*. *France, late 15th century*

34

The loom is stretched by means of a winch

Gobelins high-warp tapestry. Tracing of the design[3]

Before weaving the high-warp weaver has to sketch the design on the warp threads. He makes a full-sized tracing of the design . . .

Pierre Daquin, Devenant *(detail)*. *1969. Saint-Cyr workshop*

. . . and places the tracing-paper in front of the warp

Then, sitting behind the threads, looking at the tracing against the light, the high-warp weaver sketches the design onto the threads using a sharpened wood stick dipped in ink

5 WEAVING

The rod shed

The weaver, reaching above the leashes, pulls back the odd set of warp threads with his left hand. He holds the bobbin between the thumb and forefinger of his right hand, to the right of the pulled-back threads

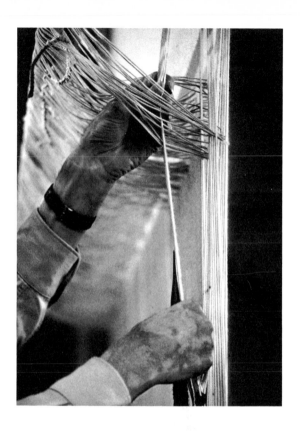

The weaver passes his fingers through the shed with a brisk downwards movement from right to left, his thumb and the bobbin staying on the outside. The bobbin is then held to the left of the threads, head down, point in the air

The weaver swings the bobbin to catch it behind the odd set of warp threads

The weaver then brings the bobbin back through the shed,
from left to right, his thumb only remaining on the outside
of the threads

The bobbin is through

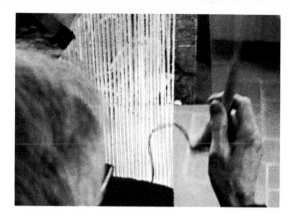

He then **beats** *it down with the point of the bobbin*

The weaver pulls the weft thread tight

History of King Clovis *series. Head of a dead soldier (detail). Arras style, middle 15th century*

The leash shed

The weaver lets go of the odd threads and pulls down on the appropriate leashes to pull back the even threads

As for the rod shed the bobbin is held horizontally in the right hand between thumb and fingers and to the right of

44

the threads pulled back by the leashes; but this time the bobbin is placed in the shed immediately

The weaver passes the bobbin briskly through the shed from right to left, his thumb sliding over the outside of the threads. He swings the bobbin towards his thumb and slides it back over the outside of the threads while his fingers move back through the shed

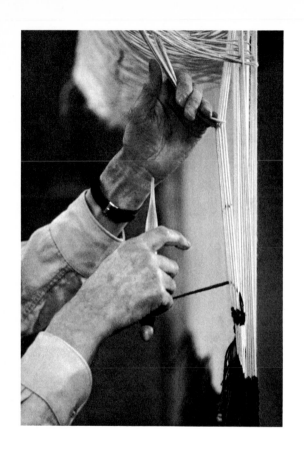

The second pick is completed

The high-warp weaver at work. He sits behind the loom, lit from the front, with the model behind him

The bobbins hanging behind the tapestry cannot fall; they are held by a slip-knot

The high-warp weaver carefully beats down the weft with the point of the bobbin

The Passion *series*. The Crucifixion and Scenes from the glorious Life of Christ *(detail)*. *Arras style, early 15th century*

The tapestry is cut from the loom

The completed tapestry ends up rolled round the upper roller, its bottom edge is cut free. When unrolled the warp threads above the tapestry are cut

6 THE LOW-WARP LOOM

We describe below the various operations in low-warp weaving inasmuch as they differ from high-warp weaving. The result – fabric made on a low-warp loom – is of course basically the same.

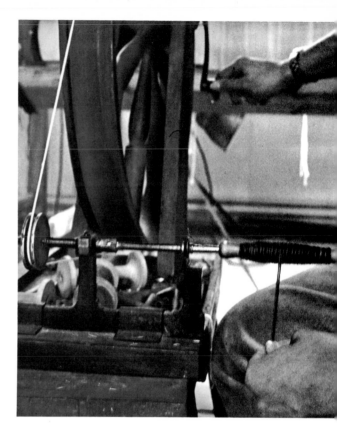

Winding the shuttles. *The winding wheel with a spool.*
These tools are not particular to the low-warp loom

Shuttles are used instead of bobbins for low-warp weaving.
Here a low-warp weaver is loading a shuttle with wool

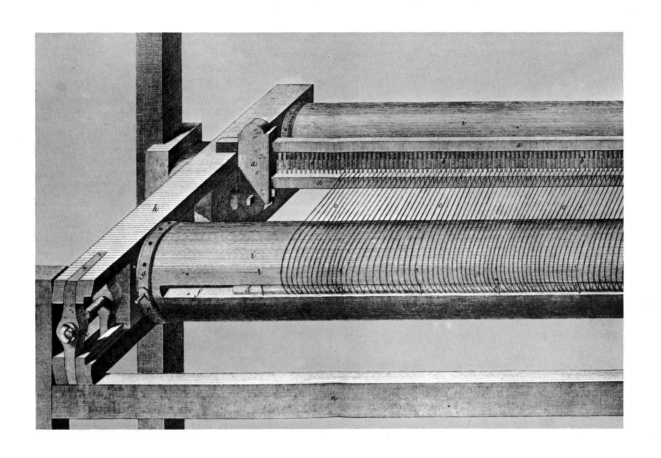

Gobelins low-warp tapestry. Perspective view of the reed on the big loom[3]

53

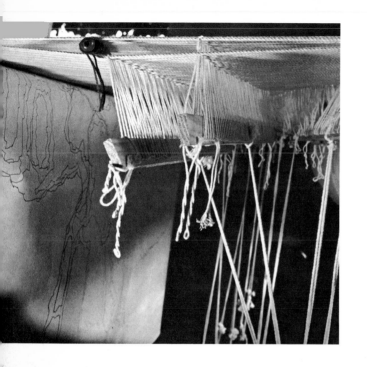
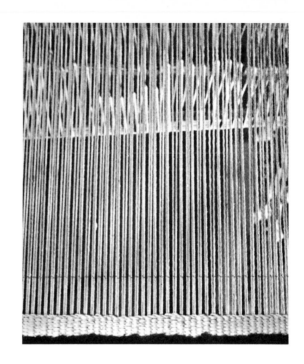

A low-warp loom seen from under the warp. All the warp threads are attached to leashes. The even thread leashes and the odd thread leashes are attached to separate rods pulled down by pedals. On this particular loom there

54

A low-warp workshop (the workshop of Pierre Daquin at Saint-Cyr-sur-Arque). In the foreground a low-warp loom is being set up (p. 56–57)

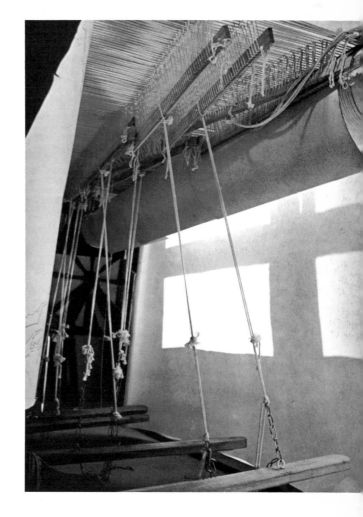

are additional leashes, as on a cloth-weaving loom, which make possible a variety of combinations of weft

The first shed is made by pressing down on a pedal. The weaver passes the shuttle through the shed with his left hand, catches it with his right hand and pulls it so that the weft thread remains between the two sets of warp threads: the first pick is completed. The weaver releases the first pedal and applies pressure to the second, so that the two sets of threads are inverted to make the second shed, he then passes the shuttle back through the second shed with his right hand, catching it and pulling it through with his left hand: the second pick is completed

The low-warp weaver beats down the weft with a comb

7 HISTORY OF TAPESTRY

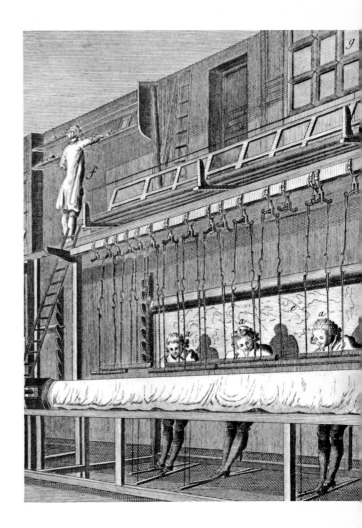

Gobelins low-warp tapestry. The workshop and various different operations[3]

Orant, *Coptic weaving.*
Late 4th century

Origins

I imagine that as Man learned very early on to protect his body from the cold with the help of skins or vegetable matter, he probably soon began to find pleasure in adorning himself, and to want to be elegant. After all the difference between Adam's fig-leaf and today's fashions is minimal. From protecting and adorning the body to decorating the dwelling-place the step must have been quickly taken. With the stretching of animal skins across cave entrances to prevent draughts hangings were invented; they were soon to be woven.

Tapestry, with its simple technique, patient work and immediate usefulness has been practised in the Orient and later in pre-Columbian America since ancient times. We will review briefly the many thousand years of its history and then deal with works of our time, as the object of this book is to contribute towards the creation of tomorrow's tapestries.

The oldest tapestries, woven by the Egyptians several thousand years ago, have not reached us. We know of their existence through pictorial representations of looms and fragments of linen material which prove that the Egyptians understood the technique of the horizontal loom as early as 3000 B.C., whereas high-warp only made its appearance during the New Kingdom. The Babylonians too decorated their buildings with monumental weavings; as can be learned from certain bas-reliefs and the ecstatic reports of Latin poets who had seen the wall-hangings of Babylon and Nineveh.

We need look no further than the examples provided by Penelope and Ovid's *Metamorphoses,* which have already been mentioned, to see that the Greeks and Romans practised a technique that has hardly altered since, and decorated their villas and palaces with tapestries and sometimes embroideries. Pliny tells us that Nero and Scipio paid merchants fabulous sums for the purchase of these hangings. An essential link in this history is supplied by the weavings of the Copts, firstly because numerous fragments have been preserved for us in the Egyptian necropolises, and secondly because they are a sort of transition between Antiquity, Byzantium and Mediaeval Europe. Coptic art – Copts is the name given by the Arabs to the earlier inhabitants of Egypt whom they found on their arrival in 640 A.D. – developed under the Pharaohs and remained active throughout the Roman period to become intimately fused with the history of the first Christians of the Nile. While resisting Moslem strictness it absorbed a whole range of influences including those of Hellenistic Egypt, Sassanian Persia, Byzantium and finally Islamic stylisation. Numerous museums have collections of Coptic fabrics, often made up of linen warp and woolen weft. The most ancient – a collection of ornamental squares – is at the Hermitage, Leningrad. Their author, even at that early date, was able to give his work a relief effect by making use of shading and hatching.

Fragments of brightly coloured material have also been found in tombs dug in the sands of the Peruvian coasts, they are made with cotton or wool thread (llama, alpaca, vicuna or guanaco wool). The oldest of these fabrics, which come from the south of the country (from the regions of Nazca and Paraca, and Chimu further north), date from the beginning of the Christian era to about the 8th century. The art then spread to the north of the country, where the subjects represented were often realistically treated animals, whereas in the southern regions a very sharp geometric stylisation is found. The fineness of the work – there are often more than 150 picks per inch – is remarkable considering how primitive the looms were. A good idea of the looms can be had from drawings on vases and also from those still used today by the Indians in different regions of South America.

Finally there are Chinese tapestries (called K'o-sseu) which date from the 8th century, although the art was certainly practised much earlier. Both the warp and weft are silk.

Chinese weavers making decorative panels used to copy paintings which often represented flowers and animals. But, thanks to their exceptional skill and the intrinsic qualities of silk, to which they later added gold and silver thread, they surpassed their cartoons and produced works of great originality.

It is impossible to tell whether tapestry and its appreciation were introduced to Mediaeval western Europe by merchants

Peruvian weaving (fragment). 1300–1450

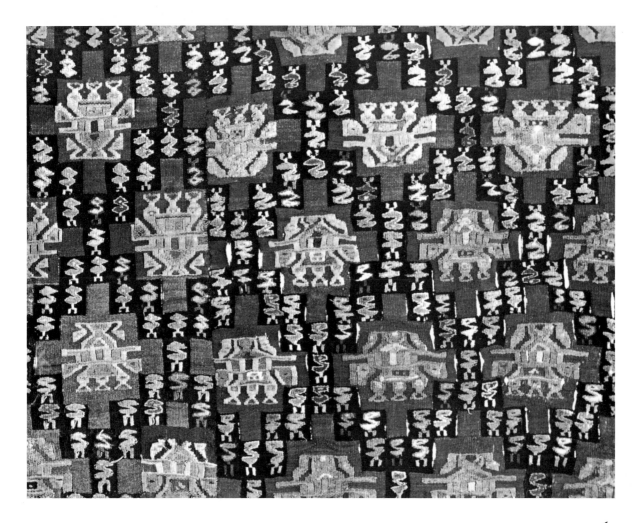

The Months. *April (fragment). Norway, early 13th century*　　　　　　　　The Months. *April (detail)*

64

importing decorative fabrics or by those great pillagers the Crusaders, who did see marvellous woven material in the East and perhaps brought some home. Nevertheless, European churches and convents were already decorated with hangings that had been made on the spot, as several texts point out.

The Middle Ages

The first question that springs to mind is: what was the function of tapestry in the Middle Ages? According to texts of the time it would appear that the oldest tapestries were most often used to decorate churches and convents. However, these sources are imprecise: do they refer to embroideries, brocades, decorated material or real tapestries? Also, it must be admitted, despite a general opinion to the contrary, that the written records, few of which date from earlier than the beginning of the 14th century, mention tapestries whose subjects are more often profane than sacred. And the fact is that at this period the Gothic style opened up church walls, piercing them with large stained-glass windows, while palaces were still narrow-doored fortresses, with only minute high windows and fire-places to break the flat surfaces of the walls of their rooms of state. The relatively large number of religious works still intact is due to their safety in convents compared to the dangerous and destructive conditions to which profane works were exposed. Tapestries were appreciated because they could be treated like mobile frescos. They were eminently portable, and our grand lords were, in a way, like sumptuous nomads: they carried their furniture with them from one castle to the next when they went a warring, ostentatiously imposing their law or raising taxes. Nevertheless, it did happen that tapestries were commissioned to fit the walls they were intended to decorate exactly. This explains the varying heights and widths that can sometimes be seen on different panels of the same hanging. However, royal accounts, those of Charles VI of France for instance, which list at each of the numerous halting points orders for nails and hooks to hang tapestries, almost make it possible to map the

The Apocalypse *series*. The Revelation of St. John ▷ *(letters to the seven churches of Asia). Paris, late 14th century*

66

itineraries of royal tourism. It is easy to imagine the arrival of the Court: the heavy rolls of wool being unloaded from carts or mules' backs, then unrolled and hung on the walls without much ceremony, instantly recreating a gay, lively and familiar decor. Creating too, depending on the season, a certain amount of warmth if a smaller "tapestry room", more practical to heat and live in, was cut off from the rest of a large hall. So much moving, especially in time of war, explains why the tapestries changed hands so often: they were part of the plunder. A tapestry belonging to Charles le Téméraire, duc de Bourgogne, for example, was seized by the Swiss and can now be seen at the Historical Museum in Berne. These removals and changes of ownership were often fatal: tapestries were lost or cut up to fit new walls, they all wore more quickly.

The Apocalypse. The beast of the earth and the beast of the sea *(detail). Paris, late 14th century*

The Apocalypse. River flowing from the throne of God and watering Paradise *(detail). Paris, late 14th century*

68

69

In these conditions it is understandable that tapestry was a luxury art, an art for such patrons as the Church and the aristocracy. The monumental weavings sometimes demanded two or three years' work; they were expensive, costing on occasion several thousand *livres*. This we know from contemporary account books which are invaluable if we want a true picture of the period. The accounts also give interesting details of the technical precision of the commissions, for instance this one given to a supplier of the ducs de Bourgogne: "To Pasquier Grenier, merchant weaver, living at Tournay, for several pieces of tapestry, worked in thread, in wool and in silk, furnished with canvas, fringes, cords and ribbons, containing in all seven hundred ells or there abouts; that is to say six wall tapestries to decorate a hall, made and worked with the history of King Assuerus."

These details of price, value and work invite a closer examination of the documents to discover what technique was used. It was long supposed, for instance, that the oldest tapestry known in the West, that of St. Gereon of Cologne, woven around

Tapestry of the coat of arms of the Duke of Burgundy (detail). Brussels, 1466

70

Symbolic Monsters *series. Woman with Basilisk (fragment). Upper Rhine, middle 15th century*

The Virgin in Glory *(detail). Brussels, 1480*

1200, of which fragments were sold by a priest to museums in Nuremberg, London and Lyon, was of Byzantine or Coptic origin. It is now thought to have come from some workshop in Rhineland. In other words, we know nothing of the origins of weaving technique in this part of the world, except that during the 12th and 13th centuries there certainly existed high-warp and low-warp looms using wool for both warp and weft. Later, weavers at Arras demonstrated their greater refinement by adding gold and silk threads and a warp of vegetable thread to the traditional wool. They had their wool dyed between fifteen and twenty pure, frank colours – no more. These, unfortunately, faded as the centuries passed. The reds and blues, extracts of madder and woad, were relatively fast; for this reason they are the dominating colours in the few 14th century tapestries that have come down to us, but the three colour harmony of these tapestries is misleading for we must imagine next to it the bright greens and violets and es-

The Offering of his Heart. *Arras workshops, early ▷ 15th century*

Episodes from Hercules' Childhood. *Tournai style, circa 1480*

pecially yellows, which came from dyer's weed, a variety of reseda, which have almost completely disappeared, as have the browns which were extracted from bark. The development of the spinning and dyeing industries in Flanders was undoubtedly responsible for the creation of the centres where tapestry-making grew: Arras, Tournai, and then Brussels. The influence of these towns through the prodigious progress of tapestry-making was such that, by a well-known process of assimilation, the Italians applied the name of the town Arras to tapestry, which they still call "arazzo". Their work could be quite fine – eighteen threads per inch can be counted in the verdure of "aux armes de Bourgogne" at the Berne Historical Museum, which was made in Brussels in 1466. Or it could be coarser, with only ten or thirteen threads per inch in many other tapestries. This probably depended on the price that the client was prepared to pay rather than the skill of the craftsman or the tradition of the atelier.

The existence of high-warp workshops has been traced in all the Flanders centres and in Paris. They followed the fortunes of the

The Justice of Trajan and Herkinbald *(fragment)*.
Arras style, middle 15th century

75

kings of France, that is to say that they shifted to the Loire region during the English conquest, and then to the Germanic countries, essentially to Rhineland and up to Switzerland. It would be hazardous, however, to make a map of other workshops. Their master-weavers might well move from place to place depending on the commissions they hoped to receive.

We reproduce here a few tapestries of the time which can only give an idea of the blossoming of themes and subjects during the Gothic period. The draughtsmen whose models served as guides for the weavers were, at the outset, more often inspired by illuminations of manuscripts than by paintings. It seems, however, that most of the time the weavers did the drawing themselves – a practice which the painters did not appreciate, as the attacks levelled at weavers by the Brussels painters in 1476 clearly suggest. An agreement followed which still left the weavers considerable autonomy. It is difficult to determine the

The Hercules Cycle *series*. The Conquest of the Island of Sheep *(detail)*. *Tournai, late 15th century*

The Adoration of the Magi, *Arras style, middle* ▷ *15th century*

degree of freedom either exercised, but the painter, sometimes himself a weaver, must have played an important role in the composition, be it a simple early work with few figures or an elaborate 15th century design. His work was probably restricted to the presentation of a drawing containing some greys and a few indications of colour. Anyway, the difference between telling a story by means of an illuminated manuscript and narrating it on a tapestry, which could be 158 yards long by 6 yards high, like the Angers *Apocalypse,* is so great, and the limitations so different, that we can safely assume that the weaver's art was more or less autonomous and to a very large extent creative. Tapestries held a mirror to the events and society of their time – as seen by the rich, naturally, which means a prettying mirror. Yet they give us a fascinating insight on the details of clothing and furnishings, on work and on leisure at the end of the Middle Ages. Think of all the subjects captured in their weft: the *Apocalypse,* for instance – so apt a subject, considering

The Court of Venus *series (detail). Arras style, second half of 15th century*

The Glorification of Christ. *Brussels, late 15th cen-* ▷ *tury, early 16th century*

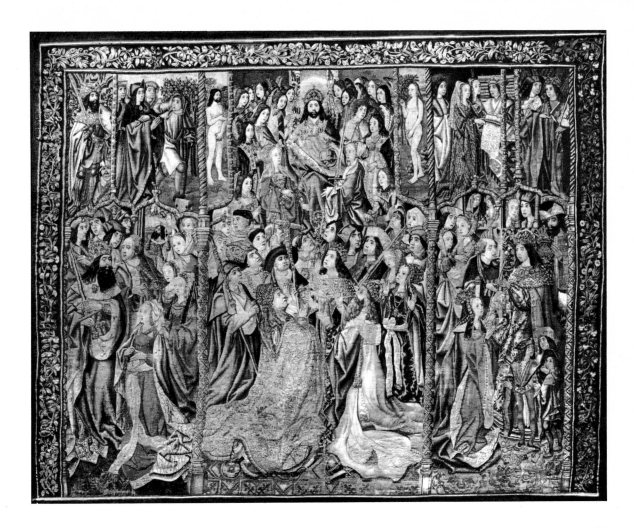

the troubles of the time – or episodes lifted from the life-histories of local saints and martyrs, or scenes taken from the New and Old Testaments, antique myths, the lives of the heroes, romances of courtly love, or again purely decorative subjects such as coats of arms and *Mille Fleurs;* then, at the time of the first great discoveries, exotic themes; sometimes even plain themes as in the Oslo *Monthly Tasks,* a fragment of which, *Woodcutters,* Madame de Sévigné may well have had in mind, many years later – such was the popularity of these subjects still – when she wrote in a letter: "I occupy my time pleasantly by having great trees felled; the commotion this causes is a real-life version of those tapestries where winter tasks are represented: people sawing, others piling logs, yet others loading carts, and in the middle – your humble servant. You can imagine the picture."

Focillon believed that: "The art of high-warp tapestry was for the West the equivalent of the Italian fresco. Together with

The Grape Harvest *(fragment). Loire workshops (?), late 15th century*

The Lady with the Unicorn *series.* Taste. *Loire* ▷ *workshops (?), late 15th century*

Landscape with animals. Brussels (?), middle 16th century

The Woodcutters (fragment). Arras style, late 15th century

stained-glass it is the most original expression of Western European genius. Towards the 15th century, tapestries in our churches displayed a comprehensive tableau of human life, from the Creation to the Last Judgement. In it historical allusions and events mingle with teachings from the Gospels...."

Middle Ages tapestry was indeed an accomplishment. By at once serving, incorporating and transposing the other arts: architecture, painting, drawing, miniatures, history, poetry and romances, it succeeded, within the context and the technical limitations of the period, in achieving what contemporary artists are looking for in today's

The Hunts of Maximilian *series*. June *(detail)*.
Brussels workshops, circa 1530

The Hunts of Maximilian. February

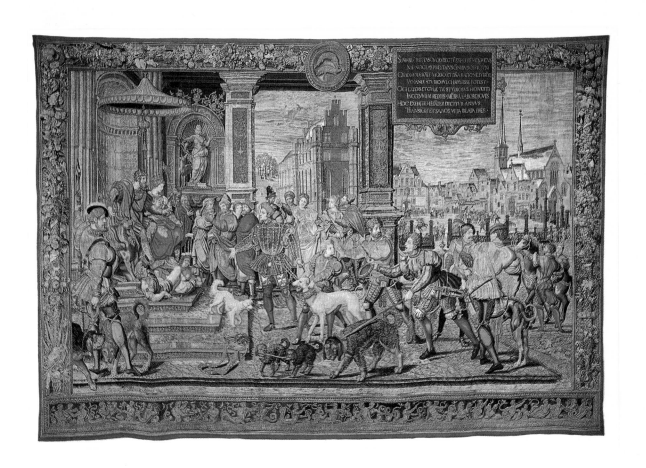

85

The Hunts of Maximilian *(detail)*. *Head of Charles V*

chaotic atmosphere, being – as they are – no longer interested in "Paintings" or "Sculptures", but in "Objects", "Environments" and "Conceptual Art", and even proclaiming that Art is dead – a belief which, hopefully, should lead to something new: an Art for everyone by everybody.

The Renaissance

On 15 June 1515, Raphael received a first payment on account for a commission by Pope Leo X for ten tapestry cartoons illustrating the *Acts of the Apostles* to decorate the side-walls of the Sistine chapel. With the help of his pupils John of Udine and Franscesco Penni he completed the cartoons towards the end of 1516, and received the balance of his fee on the 15 December of the same year. Pope Leo X entrusted the Brussels master-weaver Pietr Van Edinghen, called Pietr Van Elst with the weaving of the tapestries. The master-weaver was commissioned simply to copy the cartoons. It took him three years, and at Christmas 1519 seven panels were ready to hang at the Vatican. The execution itself, that is to say the copying of Raphael's cartoons, was supervised by yet another artist, probably Bernard Van Orley, a romanized Flemish painter, aided by Tomaso Vincitore. A certain heaviness seems to have crept into Raphael's design as a result of weaving; obviously the weaver did not give in easily, he could not, for instance, resist adorning Christ with a spangled robe, as was traditional in tapestry, although Raphael had left it as a large white area. The stipulations of the commission must have seemed indeed extraordinary to the Flemish craftsmen. Not only were they presented with a design of an entirely unfamiliar character, but they were denied the freedom to interpret it. In Rome, however, the tapestry was a great success. It was a Raphael all right, but a Raphael magnified and made monumental by the wool, like a new sort of fresco. A fashion was launched, a new style that heralded a new period in the history of tapestry. The fame of the "promoter" and of the "designer" of the work, as Pope Leo X and Raphael might have been called these days, no doubt played an important part in the success, but there was more to it than that. There was something new in the air, a certain predilection of the Italian Renaissance for painting which

Arithmetic *(fragment)*. *France, early 16th century*

History of Artemisa *series*. Heralds on Horseback
(fragment). *Paris, early 17th century*

made it the supreme art, a predilection which was imposed all over Europe by the courts of Charles V and Philip II of Spain, and Francis I and Henry II in France.

From then on tapestry was so subjected to painting that it was usually framed. The traditional narrow borders widened, filled with grotesque motifs and became an important part of the composition. These cartoons were re-edited several times – in Brussels, in England, and in France at the Gobelins and at Beauvais. It can be said that they set a trend the influence of which was to be felt in thousands of tapestries down to the 1940's.

The pervasiveness of this influence is also due to the importance of the Brussels workshops and the quality of their work at a time when the Arras studios were bankrupt and the Paris ateliers dispersed.

The Renaissance, with its sparkling new castles and novel luxuries created a new clientele for tapestry among the aristocracy but also among the bourgeoisie whose members, in their new affluence, were building themselves expensive town houses, a development which seems to be corroborated by Ronsard's advice: "You should follow the example of good housekeepers who hang their halls, bedchambers and offices with tapestry...."

Flemish workshops reached the peak of their glory during the first third of the 16th century. Above all Brussels, surrounded by a constellation of lesser centres: first Tournai, then Bruges, Enghien, Audenarde, Valencienne, Lille and Gand. Work from each centre bore a distinguishing mark – these became compulsory in 1528 – for instance BB for Brussels, a B in a crown over a bobbin for Bruges, a crenelated tower for Tournai and spectacles for Audenarde. But these marks have often been lost with the wear and tear of the tapestries' borders. Brussels supplied the "big" clients: the Regents of Austria, Charles V and Philip II of Spain, and it was the town where the best specialists were found as well as the painters who had learned to collaborate with them; skills were handed down from father to son. It was there, in fact, that the craft was best organized and its interests best protected.

Italian influence, then, was not felt as a brutal colonization. The two styles merged gradually until artists started producing

The Months *or* Royal Houses *series*. September, the Château de Chambord *(fragment)*. *Paris, Gobelins, late 17th century*

Cartoon by Toussaint Dubreuil for the Story of Diana
(see p. 91)

(see p. 91)

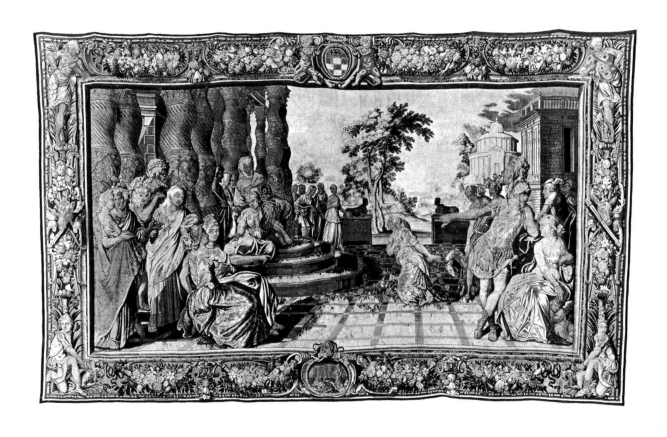

The Story of Diana *series*. Diana imploring Jupiter or an Assembly of the Gods. *Paris, Faubourg Saint-Marcel workshops, early 17th century*

The Story of Don Quixote *series*. The Theft of the Donkey *(fragment)*. *Paris, Gobelins, late 18th century*

veritable paintings in the guise of cartoons and weavers became willing to transpose any painting in wool. After the *Acts of the Apostles* the weavers worked for Giulio Romano, notably, and other pupils of Raphael. The design became more emphatic, the horizon line was lowered so that the composition came to ressemble more closely an Italian painting while mythological subjects became increasingly frequent.

Decadence set in on the death of Charles V. It had many causes – economic, political and artistic all inextricably linked and brought about, in general, by the mismanagement of the occupying Spanish.

At the same time some Flemish weavers, summoned by Italian princes, left their country to found workshops, often ephemeral, in various towns in Italy, the best known ones still being at Ferrara, Florence and Mantova. Others, many of them fleeing Spanish persecution, installed themselves in Germany, England, Sweden or Denmark.

In France, after the great dispersal noted above, the countryside had been dotted with ateliers, some of them for the first time in the region of Aubusson. Certainly the most important event of the 16th century was the foundation of the first royal factories, a move in keeping with the national policy of centralization enforced by all French kings until the Revolution.

These factories played such a positive role that it was not without due cause that the academician Louis Gillet wrote, paradoxically enough: *Gillet's law: All great French painting up to David,* that is to say until around 1780, *has been tapestry.*(. . .) There is but one really homogeneous tradition in France, only one painting movement developing according to its own laws and demonstrating visible continuity: the tapestry tradition. Tapestry in France is the major channel of artistic expression, the great popular, national current of art until the revolution caused by David's *les Horaces et les Sabines. . . .*

Francis I set up the first of his factories at Fontainebleau. It was productive for about fifteen years around 1540 and 1550. His aim was to have the hangings he needed woven there, while imposing his own style, the style of the Italians at Fontainebleau who popularized the representation of architecture in their compositions. Henry II, who had probably seen the Fontainebleau ateliers at work, established a new workshop at the Hôpital de la Trinité in Paris, a sort of professional training centre which employed one hundred and thirty-six

The Loves of the Gods *series.* Mars and Venus. *Beauvais workshops, middle 18sh century*

orphans and abandoned children. It was active until the middle of the 17th century. Finally, Henry IV was to go even further in what was in fact one of the many aspects of the liquidation of traditions inherited from the Middle Ages. Henry II had already scandalized the private ateliers by granting his orphans rights which violated the rules of the guilds. Henry IV, who is reported to have shown interest in the Trinité workshop and advocated the development of industries in his kingdom, organized a new workshop in 1597, in a Paris house that had once belonged to the Jesuits. In 1605 he transferred it to the Louvre, where he even lodged the master-weavers. Turning to the faster method in order to increase output, he had Flemish low-warp weavers come to Paris in 1601, in spite of complaints from local high-warp weavers; he installed them in the St. Marcel district, in buildings that had been the property of an old family of dyers, the Gobelins. In 1607 Henry IV granted his Flemish protégés – Marc de Cosmans and Frank Van der Planken – advantages that amounted to little less than a monopoly and a number of privileges which must have seemed outrageous to supporters of the old guild system. He lodged them at his own expense along with their two hundred workmen to whom he granted French citizenship and whom he exempted from all taxes. As for the two masters, he had an allowance paid to them, reimbursed their installation costs and gave them titles of nobility. They, in return, promised to get eighty looms working, sixty in Paris and twenty in Amiens. The foundations were thus laid for what was to become the great Manufacture royale des Gobelins.

So we reach the dawn of the 17th century with the two most outstanding developments in the history of tapestry during the Renaissance accomplished: mediaeval traditions are scorned and have been abandoned for ever, while in a number of countries princes, and in France the king himself, have established workshops where tapestries are woven which illustrate the subjection of this form of art to painting.

The 17th century
During the first half of the 17th century Flemish tapestry, a powerful industry still, declined fatally. Its most skilled experts continued to be drained abroad. The fate of the two most important centres, Brussels and Audenarde, best illustrates this decadence. In the former, at the beginning of the century, there were a hundred odd

craftsmen employing nearly 1500 workers. There were only eight left in 1700. In the latter, a census in 1654 showed that there were still a thousand craftsmen; thirty years later, after the bombardment of the town, they were all gone.

Even the weighty collaboration of Rubens could not check the decline, although orders due to the reputation of the Anvers master may have slowed it down a bit.

Rubens' intrusion into the industry caused a minor technical revolution: he painted his compositions himself and then had them blown up by his pupils not in distemper but in *oils*. This created no mean problem for the weavers: how to render in wool the master's brushwork with its transparent effect and light subtly reflected on flesh. Because what counts in Rubens' work is the figures in the foreground and their movement; the usual decorative elements disappear except for an architectural background. Rubens didn't believe in the tales he illustrated. His robust world of gods and heroes, vice and virtue, is a world

The Hunts of Louis XV *series*. The King holding a Bloodhound *(fragment)*. *Paris, Gobelins, middle 18th century*

once removed, a mere pretext for painting, for turning paint into flesh. He even used tapestries as subjects for his tapestries. Thus in *Triumphs,* episodes from the Old Testament can be seen on hangings stretched between two wreathed columns – an example of the baroque taste of the time which was cultivated by his followers, Jordaens and Téniers, whose straight-forward, less pretentious works were long in keen demand.

Rubens helped lead the Flemish weavers into an impasse. The new cartoons demanded a virtuosity entirely unsuited to the characteristics of their materials; they got around this with varying degrees of success by increasing the colour range, making excessive use of hatching and giving up the usual superb juxtapositions of tone. The colours of their poorly dyed wools turned out badly and dulled unequally.

Flemish weavers haunted foreign towns more than ever before. Among the many workshops where they handed on their techniques and even imposed their vocabulary the Mortlake factory, established in 1619 by James I of England after Henry IV's example in Paris, produced work of lasting value. James I hired fifty first-rate Flemish specialists whose business he subsidized generously, permitting them to use their ability to the full if not to innovate.

In 17th century Italy the most influential atelier was that set up in Rome by Cardinal Francesco Barberini around 1630 under the direction of a Frenchman. The cardinal, a rich and cultured collector of antiques, managed to persuade excellent painters like Pietro da Cortona to make cartoons on antique themes clearly identifiable as such but renewed by baroque taste and comprehensible in the context of contemporary history. In fact this workshop took over from the Medici's studios in Florence, although it hardly survived the cardinal's death in 1679.

In Paris it was a painter once again – Simon Vouet – who most influenced tapestry during the first half of the 17th century. Louis XIII recalled Vouet from Italy in 1627 "to ornament the royal mansions and for the new tapestry factories that His Majesty intends shoulds flourish". Vouet coloured his large compositions, which were enriched by magnificent borders, in the lively Italian manner. Other well-

The Turkish ambassador leaving the Tuileries
gardens after an audience with the King. *Paris,
Gobelins, middle 18th century*

97

known painters of the time worthy of mention here as the authors of projects for hangings are: Philippe de Champaigne, Lesueur and Sébastien Bourdon. There were active workshops at Amiens, Tours and Reims. More important still, studios were created at Maincy by the great financier Nicolas Fouquet, the financial secretary, who very wisely put at their head the painter Charles Le Brun, whose talent for sumptuous decoration was particularly well-suited for tapestry.

The impetus given at Fontainebleau by Francis I a century earlier culminated in 1662 in Colbert's purchase, in the name of Louis XIV, of what was, strictly speaking, the town mansion of the Gobelins family, along with several outbuildings. Colbert, who was to become Superintendant of the King's Buildings in 1664, installed there the Maincy studios, whose protector Fouquet had fallen into disgrace, along with the various high-warp and low-warp workshops of Paris which he decided to regroup under the same roof. Charles Le Brun was appointed director of the new institution in 1663; in 1667 it was renamed *Manufacture royale des Meubles de la Couronne*. It gathered together not only weavers, but members of all the arts and crafts: painters, sculptors, cabinet-makers, mosaicists, metal-founders and gold and silversmiths. From then on, with the exception of early works from the Beauvais ateliers, the history of the Gobelins, charged with celebrating the glory of the absolute monarch, became one with the history of French tapestry – the name was in fact synonymous with tapestry for the next three centuries.

Like Rubens, Le Brun gave up using cartoons painted in distemper. He drew small sketches which were completed by his pupils as full-sized oil-paintings; these were then cut into strips about a yard wide which were easier to handle. It was a real industry with the division of labour that the term implies: some painters and weavers concentrated on architectural details, others on flowers and fruit, yet others on landscape or figures. In addition to artists and master-weavers, two hundred workers and about sixty apprentices were employed at the Gobelins. Fame had come at last to the Manufacture, but events apparently unrelated to the arts were soon to make themselves felt again. In 1694 state finances

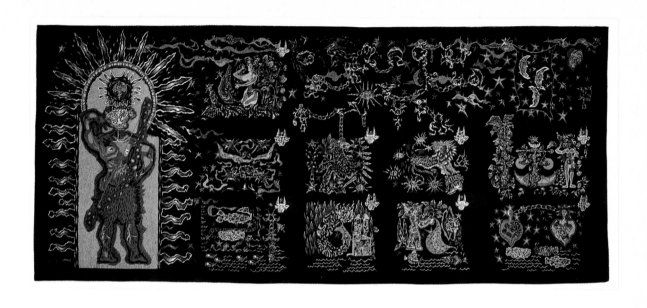

Jean Lurçat, Le Chant du Monde *series*. Poetry. *1961.*
Aubusson workshops

ran into trouble and the establishment, then run by Mignard, had to close down for five years. A number of its workmen managed to find work at the royal factory at Beauvais, which had been founded in 1664. Beauvais, a private business subsidized by the state, worked for both the aristocracy and the bourgeoisie and kept the Flemish tradition alive in France. The workshops at Aubusson and Felletin also became royal factories at the same time, but they never played a major role.

The 18th century

When the Gobelins looms started working again in 1699 the man in charge was a former director of Beauvais, the animal-painter Jean-Baptiste Oudry. He was a man well-suited to his century. Like his predecessors, he has been reproached with carrying even further the subjection of tapestry to painting. All the same, he was the man responsible for a certain change of taste. He may not have been the prime cause of this change, but at least he was the agent for it in his own sphere. Following the lead of France the whole of Europe caught the new mood and moved away from acade-

mism. 18th century tapestry was a likeable, frivolous art, rarely religious or pompous. It was intended to please, pictures in wool were fitted into the paneling and repeated on furniture. Keeping up with the fashion implied a continual self-renewal, an endless search for new subjects. François Boucher produced the most graceful results. But it is perhaps a sign of the times that the workers, who were always being asked for more – at the end of the 18th century they had to work with more than a thousand colours compared to the fifteen or twenty of the 14th century – managed to obtain fixed salaries instead of being payed for piece-work.

This brings us to the end of the 18th century: it was the century of the French, it was their turn to set up workshops abroad, as far afield as Munich and St. Petersburg.

Rendered oblivious of the rest of the world by our Westernism we have hardly lifted our eyes from Europe so far. A quick glance outside our continent, however, shows us that the Peruvians continued to

Jagoda Buic, Hommage to Pierre Pauli *(fragment).*
1970–71, Zagreb, the artist's studio

weave fine tapestries in which Indian and Spanish motifs met happily, while in China the *K'o-sseu* tapestries that dropped off the looms were more and more stylized. Soon, in the 19th century, high-lights in paint appeared with increasing frequency – a sure sign of decadence in the original art of tapestry.

The French Revolution came along and burned a few royal tapestries hoping to recover their gold thread. In that sombre and smouldering period this was a very minor incident, but the perennial symbol gold was to survive it all.

The 19th century
The revolution urged weavers to extol "those men who deserve well of Mankind". Napoleon ordered them to weave his legend. Meanwhile the pace of history was accelerating and soon the chemists, the sorcerers of the 19th century, came into the limelight. They made the fortune of the most uninspired imitators. It was a great day for the director of the Gobelins during

Georges Henri Adam, La Dame de Cœur. *1949, Aubusson workshops*

the Restauration when His Majesty "was able to judge for himself the high degree of perfection which the art of imitating all styles had reached in his Factory". Then the great chemist Chevreul got down to work. From 1824 to 1889 he directed the *Laboratoire des teintures des Gobelins.* Thanks to him weavers had a palette of 14,400 tones at their disposal and managed to copy to the very image works by the impressionists. No need to worry though, all this soon faded into a hardly recognizable collection of dirty greys and polluted hues. The sparkling colours that were once the pride and joy of their authors gave up the ghost in less than fifty years ... The art of tapestry had never been so close to painting and never so far. Once dead it could only await rebirth. "... tapestry today is a dead art. It is no more than a dull, dark, laborious imitation of painting." This statement of failure by the Goncourt brothers in their *Journal* of 14 September 1874, was in fact being challenged at that very moment by something that was stirring in London, where the poet William Morris, a devotee of the applied arts, had grouped together painters and craftsmen to found his first

workshop in 1861. The shop soon grew in size and was subsequently transferred to Merton Abbey, near Wimbledon. Morris was passionately interested in embroidery, stained-glass, furniture, jewellery and leather-work, as well as tapestry. He had steeped himself in the spirit and tradition of mediaeval weaving. Inspired by late 15th century works he composed his own designs for proposed tapestries – they were rather like an accompanying text for draughtsmen's copies of cartoons by painters like Burne-Jones. Morris died in 1896, but his workshop carried on until 1940. He was more than an imitator. In his attempt to create a new style he proceeded systematically and analytically, proposing that the number of colours should be limited and perspective abandoned. It is perhaps worth mentioning that workshops were being set up in the United States also at this period, such as the atelier founded in 1908 by Albert Herter, a painter who wove from his own cartoons and explored the same sort of territory as William Morris. Workshops

Antonín Kybal, Hope. *Prague, the artist's studio*

opened in Germany, too, and caught the interest of the expressionist painters. Elsewhere, in Czechoslovakia, Norway and Poland, men and women, some of them influenced by folk art, others by the Middle Ages, took up weaving, giving the art of tapestry a new lease of life.

France was slow to join the movement, perhaps because academism was more solidly anchored there than elsewhere. The sculptor Maillol, however, manifested some interest in tapestry around 1890 and produced a few works of a simple straightforward design.

Contemporary tapestry
And now one feels like saying: "And Lurçat came". The way had been paved for him by the initiative of Madame Cutolli who had had a painting of Rouault's woven at Aubusson in 1932, followed by works by her favorite painters: Braque, Dufy, Picasso, Matisse, Léger, Miró, Marcoussis, Derain, Coutaud and Lurçat. While this may have brought about a rejuvenation of style it in no way altered the approach to tapestry usual at that time since some of these weavings were put behind glass and

Brit H. Warsinski, Form I. *1970. Oslo, the artist's studio*

framed. "Frankly, it was a fundamentally reactionary movement, a step back towards the 18th century", said Lurçat later.

This attempt, however, linked up as it was with such famous names, had the merit at least of making the art world realize that all was not well in the kingdom of tapestry.

Jean Lurçat, painter and poet, was a man of character and a strong personality. I like to think that it was the *feel* of the material that won him when he started working with wool in 1915, embroidering on canvas. Much later, having worked for some time at the Gobelins, he was invited to Aubusson by the director of the *Ecole des arts décoratifs*. There he met the shopforeman François Tabard in the very works where generations of the Tabard family had been labouring since 1637. Lurçat tried his hand at the loom and designed a cartoon which was woven by the students of the school. In 1937 Tabard and Lurçat decided to make a hanging of about 160 sq. feet, which they called *Harvest*. It was the first step in an experiment, better – a successful venture, whose happy effects can still be felt. The same year, which was a decisive one for Lurçat, he passed through Angers and saw the *Apocalypse*. He has described the scene: "Spiders were weaving their traps in the murky corners. The sacred cloth hung there, great nails piercing its palms."

Beatrix Sitter-Liver, Private Passage. *1971, Köniz, the artist's studio*

Luis Feito, Guadarrama. *1971. Saint-Cyr workshop*

107

Evelyn Anselevicius, Linear Face III. *1970–71. San Miguel, Mexicano workshops*

Yaacov Agam, Solfège. *1971. Aubusson, Goubely workshop*

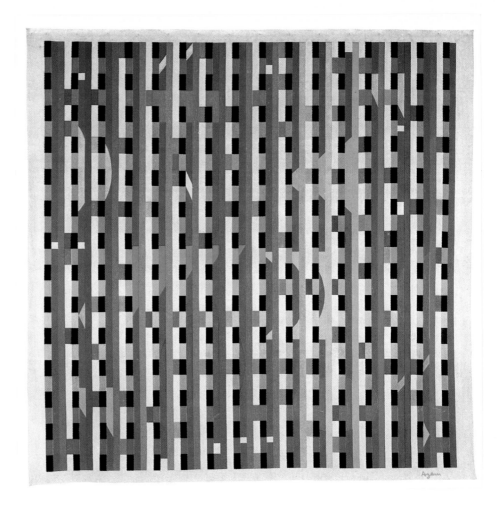

109

Pierre Daquin, Mospalis. *1968. Paris, Saint-Cyr workshop*

On Tabard's advice Lurçat decided to make wool his starting point instead of paint. He selected his hues and worked out colour scales, numbering the yellows from one to six, then the blues, the greens, the ochres, greys and reds. From then on his cartoons consisted of drawings with numerical indications. By reducing the number of colours Lurçat also reduced the cost price considerably. In 1939, Guillaume Janneau, the administrator of the Beauvais and Gobelins ateliers, decided to send him to Aubusson, where the Paris workshops had been evacuated for the war, but Lurçat was already there. He was joined by the painter Gromaire, and the moribund little town then witnessed the birth of modern tapestry. Jean Lurçat passionately undertook the weaving of over a thousand tapestries up to the *Chant du Monde* that he was working on at his death in 1966. He was the founder of a school. He launched a veritable Renaissance. On 15 June 1962 he inaugurated the first Tapestry Biennale at Lausanne which he had promoted with the patronage of CITAM (Centre international de la tapisserie ancienne et moderne), which was also his idea. The fifth Biennale took place in 1971. Some five hundred artists from thirty-four countries exhibited seven hundred and thirty-four works. Three main trends emerge which are worth discussing here:

There are those weavers who continue to copy well-known paintings, by Picasso or Chagall, say, and are solely concerned with achieving a good transposition into wool.

Then, following in Lurçat's wake there are painters who design their cartoons while "thinking" tapestry and who – ideally – collaborate with weavers and respect the rules of the craft, when they know them. Some also break new ground, like the Frenchman Pierre Daquin at his Saint-Cyr atelier. Himself a weaver, he innovates constantly and boldly although his works always remain real tapestry; he operates on two warps using – and here he is not alone – a relief effect called by the French a *bourrelet*. These weavers use wool and linen thread, but also nylon, stainless steel thread, gold, silver, copper and other synthetic threads.

Finally there are those who are both artist and weaver, who create what are still

Ritzi Jacobi, Wardrobe. *1971. Frankfurt, the artist's studio*

called tapestries for convenience sake, although this is a question of semantics. Their works are no longer even hung on walls, they have neither definition nor function. They are more like textile and metal sculptures, often combined with coarse or thick materials like rope or fur, jute or sisal-fibre. Two young pioneers in this group are Magdalena Abakanowicz from Poland and the Yugoslav, Jagoda Buic.

But the best among these artists – despite their breaking all the rules, making use of collage and assembling all sorts of unusual materials to produce works which will, no doubt, call for a new terminology – remain nevertheless bound by a certain nostalgia for weaving, if we are to judge by Jagoda Buic, who says that "there are infinite possibilities of interweaving still to be explored".

Ateliers in Catalonia, Czechoslovakia, Holland, Portugal, Switzerland and the United States should also be mentioned, but then young weavers are at work all over the world.

Magdalena Abakanowicz, Red Abakan. *1969. Warsaw, the artist's studio*

Dear Reader, you have seen tapestries, you have touched them, you have perhaps read our book as far as this page, and, who knows, you may be tempted by tapestry-weaving.

To start with we must warn you that it is a relatively expensive art. A loom will cost you from £ 100 to £ 150 pounds sterling. The cost-price of the tapestry itself depends on three factors: 1) the *cartoon*: its price depends on the quality and on the artist's reputation, unless you design it yourself; 2) *basic materials*: For a normal tapestry with the usual warp you should allow about £ 1 to £ 1.50 per pound for coloured wool, and you will need about two or three pounds per square yard of tapestry. This price will be doubled or tripled if you have your wools dyed yourself. 3) *Labour,* this is the most important thing – your work. It will vary a lot depending on your dexterity, but also on the simplicity or complexity of the cartoon. If the lines of the design follow the direction of the weft it will be easier to translate, if the lines follow the warp it will be more difficult and thus slower.

Finally, the care with which the work is done counts, as does that given to the strength of the tapestry. With a simple cartoon, a weaver, with care, can weave a bit more than two square yards a month, but more often it takes about a month or a month and a half to weave a square yard. It may cheer you up to know that in the 19th century it took a year to weave a square yard. . . . So it can cost between £ 100 and £ 250 per square yard to produce a normal tapestry, not counting the cartoon or overheads.

When your tapestry is completed don't fold it, roll it. And whatever you do, don't iron it!

To work!

113

Tapestry	The Arts	General
Egypt circa 1580 B.C.		
The technique already known during the XVIIth dynasty (fragments discovered in the tombs of Amenhotep II and Tutankhamen)	Ceramics, paintings, murals, bas-reliefs	Aryan invasion. Mycenean, Cretan, Mesopotamian civilizations
10th century B.C.		
Homer portrays Penelope weaving in the *Odyssey*	First Greek temples Jerusalem Temple	Foundation of the Kingdom of Israel
6th century B.C.		
Tapestries seen in Babylon and Nineveh	Sculpture and vase painting in Greece	Croesus, king of Lydia Cyrus, king of Persia
43 B.C. – 16 A.D.		
Ovid tells the story of Arachne's rivalry with Minerva in his *Metamorphoses*	Augustus' Forum Pompeii mosaics	Augustus emperor of Rome Tiberius emperor of Rome
Circa 1st century A.D.		
First tapestries in Peru, in the regions of Nazca and the Paraca peninsula in the south and Chimu in the north	Colosseum Gallo-Roman funeral steles	Nero, Trajan
3rd century A.D.		
First Coptic tapestries (Egypt)	Pyramid of the Sun in Central America	First Maya town

Tapestry	The Arts	General
7th–10th centuries		
Tapestries known as *K'o-sseu* appear in China	Statue of Buddha in China Charlemagne's palace at Ingelheim	Charlemagne Otto I
Circa 1260 In Paris, Etienne Boileau's *Le Livre des Métiers* records the rules of the "Saracen" weavers	Gothic art, stained glass Nicolas Pisano	Seventh Crusade Louis IX
1375 Jean de Bondolf, called Hennequin de Bruges, receives a commission from the duc d'Anjou for the hanging *The Apocalypse*. Nicolas Bataille, Parisian high-warp weaver, is asked to undertake the weaving	Gentile da Fabriano Palma cathedral Bruges town hall	Richard II king of England Great schism of the West
1386–1397	Births of: Fra Angelico, Donatello, Jan van Eyck, Paolo Ucello	Charles VI king of France Wat Tyler
1398 Tournai weavers' rules established	Birth of Pisanello Jehan d'Orléans	Dukes of Burgundy and Orléans
1402 *Story of Saint Piat and Saint Eleuthère* woven at Arras, a series destined for the Tournai cathedral	Birth of Filipo Lippi Doges' Palace decorated	French defeat at Agincourt (1415)
1418 Parisian weavers dispersed	Flemish school: van Eyck, van der Weyden, Memling	Philippe le Bon, Duke of Burgundy Joan of Arc
1449 Philippe le Bon, Duke of Burgundy, commissions the Gideon series for the Order of the Golden Fleece	15th century Florentine school Births of Boticelli, Perugino, J. Bosch	
1452 Statutes of the Brussels weavers	Birth of Leonardo da Vinci	End of the Hundred Years' War

Tapestry	The Arts	General
1466 Philippe le Bon commissions eight works with a background of small flowers carrying the duke's coat of arms from Jean de Haze, a Brussels weaver. Some of these hangings were captured with Charles le Téméraire's baggage after the defeat at Grandson in 1476. One of them can be seen today at the Historical Museum in Berne	Venetian school: Bellini, Carpaccio	Charles le Téméraire duke of Burgundy
1476 Brussels painters complain that weavers are using cartoons not designed by painters. The weavers reply that they have always done without the services of painters. An agreement follows, first step towards the control of tapestry by painters	Verrocchio: *Il Colleone*	Ferdinand V king of Aragon Burgundy War Morat
1483	Birth of Raphael	Charles VIII king of France Richard III king of England
1485 Weaving of the Louvre *The Virgin in Glory*, an example of a tapestry directly inspired by a painting		
1492	Birth of the painter Giulio Romano	The Medici at Florence
1500	Birth of Benvenuto Cellini German school: Dürer, Grünewald, Holbein, Cranach	François I king of France Charles V emperor
1528 Ruling by the Brussels Magistrate makes tapestry marks compulsory	P. Breughel Loire castles Venetian school	Luther preaches the Reform

Tapestry	The Arts	General
1551 Foundation of the Atelier de la Trinité in Paris by Henry II	Lescot: Palais du Louvre Birth of Rubens (1577)	Henry II king of France Edward VI king of England
1598 Henry IV founds the Atelier de la Maison professe des Jésuites in Paris, later transferred to the galleries of the Louvre	Mansart Births of Bernini, Rembrandt Monteverdi	Henry IV king of France James I king of England Marie de Médicis regent in France Louis XIII king of France
1619 Creation of the Mortlake factory in England by James I	Dutch school: F. Hals, Rembrandt Flemish school: Van Dyck, Téniers, Rubens	Thirty Years' War Philip IV king of Spain Louis XIV king of France Mazarin
1658 Fouquet organizes a tapestry workshop directed by Charles Le Brun at Maincy, near his Château de Vaux	Spanish school: Velasquez, Zurbaran	Cromwell dictator in England
1662 Fouquet's disgrace. Colbert moves Charles Le Brun and his weavers from Maincy to Paris and regroups them at the Gobelins with the Faubourg Saint-Marcel and Louvre galleries ateliers	Poussin: *The Seasons* French school: Callot, Poussin, Lorrain, La Tour, Le Brun	Colbert and Louvois are ministers
1664 Foundation of the Manufacture de Beauvais	Le Brun decorates the Louvre	The French and the Hungarians fight the Turks in Hungary
1665 The Ateliers d'Aubusson become royal factories		
1667 Creation of the Manufacture Royale des Meubles de la Couronne, or *Gobelins,* under the direction of Charles Le Brun	Le Nôtre: Versailles gardens	Treaty of Aachen

Tapestry	The Arts	General
1685	Births of: J. S. Bach, G. F. Haendel	Edict of Nantes revoked Peter the Great czar
1733 Jean-Baptiste Oudry becomes director of the Gobelins	Lancret, Pergolese Greuze	War of the Polish succession
1748 Conflict between Oudry and the weavers whom he obliges to copy paintings slavishly	Houdon Pigalle Rameau	
1756	Birth of Mozart	Seven Years' War
1757 Vaucanson, an engineer, invents a rocking low-warp loom	Piranese Gainsborough	Louis XVI king of France
1789 The Gobelins reorganized	David: *The Sabines*	French Revolution
1824 The physicist Chevreul directs the Gobelins dyeing laboratory and works out a palette of 14,400 tones of wool		Charles X king of France
1861 English poet William Morris founds his own workshop	Corot, Courbet, Daumier Impressionism	3rd Republic in France
1890 The sculptor Maillol weaves at Banyuls	Van Gogh: *Sunflowers*	2nd Internationale
1892– 1966 Jean Lurçat	Ecole de Paris	
1910 Natural dyes no longer used at the Gobelins		
1915 Jean Lurçat's first embroidery on canvas	Surrealism Western art evolves towards abstraction and new realism	
1962 First Tapestry Biennale at Lausanne		Cuba affair

GLOSSARY OF TECHNICAL TERMS

Basse-licier : French for low-warp tapestry weaver.

Battages : Aubusson term for non-systematic *hatching* (see hatching).

Beam bar : Metal bar in a groove which fixes the warp threads to the rollers.

Beat : To force down the weft.

Binder : Thread used to join two colours.

Bobbin : A turned wooden tool with a head one end and a point the other end; used in high-warp tapestry to pass the weft thread through the shed. The point is used to beat down the weft.

Border : A strip of plain weaving always found surrounding ancient tapestries; of practical use essentially but sometimes acting as a frame.

Cartoon : Full-sized, simplified sketch, drawn or painted, which guides the weaver during weaving; the cartoon is either placed under the warp, in the case of low-warp tapestry, or behind the weaver (usually) for high-warp tapestry; a cartoon is rendered more or less indispensable by the technique of weaving which obliges the weaver to work from detail to detail without seeing the whole and without the possibility of reworking passages.

Comb : Tool used for forcing down the weft.

Cotrets or Coterets : Gobelins term for the uprights of the loom; an ancient meaning of the word is workmates, hence perhaps its application to the two uprights.

Crenille : Aubusson term for groups of threads prepared for setting up on the loom.

Cross : Where the warp threads cross each other during warping.

Cross rod : Rod which separates the odd and even sets of warp threads in high-warp tapestry.

Dents : Spaces in the reed.

Enlevage : French term for an area woven above existing areas; it can never follow a widening form.

Fils de croisure : French high-warp tapestry term for the odd set of warp threads which remain free.

Fils de lice : French high-warp tapestry term for the even set of warp threads which are held by leashes.

Float : When one or two warp threads are left out on passing the weft. What was originally a mistake has often been used on purpose, particularly with gold and silver thread during the 16th, 17th and 18th centuries and in experiments by contemporary weavers.

Gamut : Scale of tones from light to dark, or scale of colours.

Hatching : Elongated or triangular shapes used for shading and half-tones produced by weaving proportionately increasing and decreasing numbers of picks of two tones.

Haute-licier : French for high-warp tapestry weaver.

Heddles : See *leashes.*

Hemstitching : Stiching the edges of a tapestry when cut from the loom.

High-warp : Vertical warp threads.

Jasse : French term for wool fibres which strenghten new tapestry and gradually become visible through wear and brushing.

Lac : Gobelins term for slip-knot made with weft thread by high-warp weaver to prevent bobbin from falling.

Leashes : Threads attached to the fils de lice, used to pull back the even warp threads.

Licier : French for weaver of tapestries.

Lock : To join two colours vertically with a clear division.

Low-warp : Horizontal warp threads.

Pick : A single warp thread.

Pienne : Gobelins term for a group of warp threads equivalent to 4 inches of material.

Reed : A comb which helps set the warp threads up on the loom in both high-warp and low-warp tapestry.

Rentraiture : French term for the contraction of a tapestry when cut from the loom on which it was stretched.

Rollers : The cylinders of a tapestry loom.

Shed : The opening in the warp through which the weft passes.

Shuttle : Tool used in low-warp tapestry for passing the weft through the shed.

Slit : An opening left along the warp threads when a weaver leaves two tones unattached.

Tapissier : French for weaver – now usually applied to the maker of decorative weavings rather than real tapestries.

Tracing : Drawing the design on the warp threads using tracing paper and ink.

Tracing stick : A sharpened stick dipped in ink which the weaver uses to outline the design on the warp threads.

Warp : Threads running lengthways.

Warping : Preparing the warp threads and setting them up on the loom.

Weft : Threads woven across the warp.

SELECT BIBLIOGRAPHY

Coffinet, Julien, *Arachné ou l'Art de la Tapisserie*. Geneva, 1971.

Faux, Claude, *Lurçat à haute voix*. Paris, 1962.

Guiffrey, J., *Histoire de la tapisserie depuis le Moyen Age jusqu'à nos jours*. Tours, 1886.

Jarry, Madeleine, *La Tapisserie des origines à nos jours*. Paris, 1968. (Contains a comprehensive bibliography.)

Le grand livre de la tapisserie. Lausanne-Paris, 1965.

Lurçat, Jean, *Discours de réception à l'Académie des beaux-arts*. Paris, 1965.

Lurçat, Jean, *Le travail dans la tapisserie du Moyen Age* (with a preface by Louis Gillet). Geneva, 1947.

Exhibition catalogues

Biennale de la tapisserie, Lausanne (1st, 1962; 2nd, 1965; 3rd, 1967; 4th, 1969; 5th, 1971.)

TABLE OF ILLUSTRATIONS

Government. 5th Biennale internationale
de la Tapisserie, Lausanne, Catalogue
No. 2

AUTHOR'S NOTES

[1] Homer, *The Odyssey,* translated by W.H.D.
Rouse, A Mentor Book, 1937. The authors of a
recent French translation (*L'Odyssée,* traduction et
notes de Médéric Dufour et Jeanne Raison, ed.
Garnier-Flammarion, Paris 1965) point out in a
footnote that: "It was a vertical loom. The front
and the rear were separated by wooden bars held
by hooks. The warp threads hanging outside these
bars were kept taut by means of round weights
pierced with holes. A shuttle was used to inter-
weave the weft between the warp threads, thus
making the fabric."

[2] Ovid, *Metamorphoses,* translated by Frank
Justus Miller. William Heinemann, London,
G. P. Putnam's Sons, New York, 1916.

[3] Illustration from *L'Encyclopédie de Diderot et
d'Alembert,* Paris. Librairie Panckoucke. 1786.

[4] Illustration from Boccaccio's *De claris mulieri-
bus.* Ulm 1473.

[5] Illustration from Ovid's *Metamorphoses.* Lyon,
1527.

PHOTOGRAPHIC CREDITS

The author and publisher wish to express their thanks to those who helped work on the preparation of this book; in particular: Mme Majorel and the Galerie La Demeure, Paris, Pierre Daquin and the Saint-Cyr workshop, CITAM and the Biennale de la Tapisserie, Lausanne, le Mobilier National, Paris, Mrs Erika Billeter, curator of the Bellerive Museum, Zurich, Miss Lindi Krämer, Berne, and all museums and private collectors who have been kindly made books and other documents available to us.

English version by Julian Snelling and Claude Namy.

Printed in Switzerland